Praise for *Eke*

"To eke is to create something from nothing. And Wahidah Tambee has indeed made something immense from what seems small, humble, compact. An inventive and often whimsical dive into traditions of visual and concrete poetry, this book urges acrobatic reading and adventurous swivels of sonic attention. Wahidah's kaleidoscopic poems shimmer at the edges of language, where sense becomes sensuous and shifts us away from our habits of silence and speech. Reading *Eke* during severe times, where my attention has been bludgeoned by the blunt tools of news media and punditry, I leaned against the book's capacity for bringing us closer to the clarifying, divine purposes of attentive, immersive play."

—Divya Victor, author of *Kith* and *Curb*

"To experience Nurul Wahidah's *Eke* is to wade into a sea where you don't know where the bottom is. It's mysterious, a little scary, yet very fun and welcoming. It's an expanse where words and letters are split, stretched and sutured—not to the point of nihilism but rather to realise the potential of these units as organisms in their own right—unruly, protean, and odd. They proliferate, giving birth to new shapes and new touches. How do you navigate this, or even articulate this alien ecosystem? Visually and aurally, you feel the electricity in the gaps, the fumbling and stammering which Wahidah alludes to. Whether you swim to shore, well, that's another matter altogether."

—Yeow Kai Chai,
author, *One to the Dark Tower Comes*,
and winner, Singapore Literature Prize

"Through jagged refrains, crowded pauses and visual collisions, Wahidah's words tumble pell-mell through an indexical of her own making. Here, type becomes object, object becomes breathless, and elliptical meanings quiver in the aural periphery of it all. In overlapping words and slip-spelled shapes become visible the delicious entanglements of sculpting, movement, and a sureness of poetic form. Eke is an exquisite, tantalising construction."

—Shubigi Rao,
author, *Pulp III: An Intimate Inventory of the Banished Book*, and winner, Singapore Literature Prize 2024

"Wahidah's poems remind us that reading hinges on proximity and distance, between legible words and lines, and also between illegibilities. Wahidah's creations are singularly untouchable in their assembly; they ask to beheld, and in beholding, we find in these pages both the wreckages of our divided language and a wondrous art."

—Jason Wee, author, *From A (Undesirable) Diary*

"Reading *Eke* feels like taking a magnifying glass to the given and finding that it is full of energised gaps and diversions, tensions and collisions. Wahidah's visual poems teem with life. Words meld and split apart, lines shudder and derail. We're invited into the full pleasure of the instability of language. If the poems look like clouds, it's less in their shape and more in the way they move before our eyes, dispersing, reforming, pulling us ever on towards new and unexpected evocations."

—Jennifer Crawford, author, *Koel* and *Lichen Loves Stone*

Eke

Eke

Poems

Wahidah Tambee

Published by Gaudy Boy LLC,
an imprint of Singapore Unbound
www.singaporeunbound.org/gaudyboy
New York

For more information on ordering books, contact jkoh@singaporeunbound.org.

ISBN 978-1-958652-17-6

Cover design by Flora Chan
Interior design by Jennifer Houle

To Jen and Divya

Contents

Eke

let ter s
let u s
s tell 'er
h le f t us
tell us es
let's tell
what's le f t
what s, felt s
s what's teller
a letter
a let'er
a let
let's us s h eer
s write a
letter.

in the mo ode
for a let ter
the mood to let
an alpha bet
turn into drown s
of wou r d s on a page
in mid st of sum mm oning
n umbers to b etter s w ound ing
edge
delegate s s p aces
between o f
meaning f oo ll ish
characters
make up
letters
made up
most for d st ruck
moo n umming

3

with held
by holding
on hold
to be with and
with out by
a hand hold
held away
by and by a mark

a mark of touch
withholding
to hold, by
being
held.

look,
no   f_orther than
look at me
 further than
 what other looks
can further
 look

don't
      look if can't look
  no further, further look
  no, no, no,
      further, further
      look
         at me, no, at me
         at me
         at, umm. no,
         at, umm, me

         at
      look at
      look for the
      look for them me
      look further

          for me

      look further
at me.

look
    no
look
    no further
look
    further no
look
    for the no
    further
look
    for the no further
    for the no to s$_{in}$k
look further for to
    requires
looking
    further, a little
    for the
looks to sink in
look to smile
    smiling in ssss
look, looks sink further
looks sink in, so,
look further.

eyeball
  the space
before eye.bawl
      insp e ace
      in pace
      in s pieces
      in eyede.

    bawlings ad.
        b idea.
  my eyes, s walling in
        yes s well

        yes,
        well,
    might as well
        as will a swilling
        wa i lling
    was eyes willing
      as awed bawl
        s pacing

11

c l o o k ed up
con c on fla k eable meanings
conc re t
s table
ightings
l a e thered late
inter rup ture
s
literations
fas ci tions
conc re ate na tions
pl ace ment
s t c ale

13

can t ell
by t he g u ilt y
   look of f
    t h i s ef face
      if f its really
       orn o t e lie
        or tr o u g th
      m s k e d ri inal
        wh i ch
       truly s i s it s
        glit see ing

c le_aver
a leve_el clever_{er}
le^avel l evelled
a cleaved level up
c lea^v_peable
ul^p

word s till
papers thin

hum m an t error ing
as water as blood
as b l eeding
b l l inds
evening
b r ea thing g uns

word s in
papere d still

word_still
papers_{thin}

t h err e ors

as water^{as blood}

b l inding
r ining

brims to ne
boil

word s ill
papere d in

diss miss ile
          ed
dismally
    mulled
dis tally m ust
          a
          mistily
          mask
drummed down
  d us t k

eras$_e$$_{rr}$ure dust
  ra$_z$$_{or}$^{e}d us^t
  ra$_i$$_s$ed us
erase$_a$$_d$dust
erased us

dust lies
dust lies where it should

does lie when it should be
dusted

does lie

dust it lies where it should so it
does lie where
doesn't it lie when
dust is
does it should or

dust it?

so which itch
w this t
thi s
in time
switch lines
in tit ch
saves it ?
so itches trick
w sew
t h to
inc ick
whic h es ?
so sitches itch es
w
th ick
st witches

sick?

so it seems
bias se eam binding
tapp ed off the mming
a foo ull skirt s around
wra pping
ho pen n ings out
with sound

the
hissing
stress on word issing
driving
st
inging madness
damn
in
to
mind

c l ^{t}ear ^{s}fully
meaning

s ^{t} $_w^o$ ords

which dire ct$_{ion}$

^{l}eaning
bl^{m}a$_c$$_k$

so me$_{an}$ thing
di ff ear$_{rant}$;

ma_yke

ma   ke_n
   wa_y
 s
mis^{say}ken
  t
 s ay

for ^taking
  s
     miss st^ray
    s t ^aeps
      r
    for, sakes!
      take_n over_take_n
        for ^sake n
         takes

gu e st
gae thering
gusts t
on s t aying
ly ou sting
est. es
mull t us
multi s ooths
tr
ying
to bes aid
but j ust s
g s pre a ying
sound s windling
top lease
gues s what
ay u mm
sayin g is t
gusts

of ferred
of f field
of t act
con t ext
of ferred
co n
c off i e ld ly
f m
co u gh
n g ested
i f   con tested
testi f ly
ess
of f
pro ffered
confested
con of co u rse
fussed
of ject
con sub s titute
con fort
confitude
of crude

con fli ^tting mess_{ages}
_{ck}
fleeting
^taking so_m^e_{uch}
time ticking
de^c_s iding
ub_{stan}tiating
^dard_{ising}
an s_{wearing}
dam_{nit}picking
flip_{ping} con tr^{olling}_adiction
fl_{ck}ing
p_rⁱ fli^rt_{ting}
p_lease

to get a rre solution
  e
is to re at tempt ion
   to solve
   to e
   fin d sol e ution
but to ir r esolution
is to re ab solutely
     to   le
       sa l ve
    de sol e lately

not,
  k no^w angry
    t
   no whe^re near
     a tang^le_t d
       of ang sty
       but
  ast^ra y has anger let
       ^brought burn
    a_shh tray away
      a sty of re_arr range_ing
              ra ge
          angerrange
        a_knot of   ang^st^r ay
            w roug _thing
                waves

bruntle
blurrnt sky
brooding
brontide
bwroughtonne
tideall waves
brrumbelling
thrunknelling
linking blacker
greyer shadows
sshhwoken song
thunderson
thunderstrum

im pluie
ore
im plea ding
im parting with
tears
im parti ble
cul le ar
i'm v w a oking
i'm v a ding
silence
to pro c u a re
all glistening
t ears
f o r
the s e u fferings

aScertain
direction from
landm arks
the spli gh t
Pf
between
sea
Sand
sweeping
weaves
throught cks

to _{as} say
to
to _{es}scribe
to _{in}timate _{ly}

toss ^{ay}
t ossify
^{to}s_p_a^ecification
^c _e pacifically
_sailing
^{aid}s_{eeking}
miss_{iles}

over bo a red
thro ne
surely kno wn
wh ar t's coming
cap s e i zed zure
ret treating in
s waves after
the sea t
the b o w er
top p v les

as sault tougher
salt tongued
see, sea,
g reater
to g ether.

still
mourning
stillver
rain
stalement
mate
mourn
mounttain
mournument
mnumberation

mistilled
mustinstalled

mustlet
musttrailed
musnt'rain.

and

th ^{ere} was hhh

more

not hhh ing

toss ay.

the sou^{l}nd
^{s}acre d
wakes the
pain^{t}ed days
theweaks
but does
not
sl$_i$ee$_p$
from
being

c^lou_ld I watch the morning sun^{rise}ing
rise with d^rawn
   blu ^r_e rred orange b_elow

O$_{ud}$

cl$_{ued}$ slowly

s $_{oft}$ ^{ly}

c ^{loud} ly

ou$_l$d

only shhh $_{ou}$^{l}d

^{l}oft $_l$y

s hold ^{er}

cloud oft
could^s often

li^{ke} mir_r calls
  ght_{ning} _{or}

         s_t abled _{moon}
          ill_{ver} falls
           _e

        cables of f^avour
                _{er}
                  _r

            be _{for} ^e ttune _{ment}
                _a   mo
                      _{mo}
                    _t urns
                      all.

land
the
re ams
close a
do or
ther
wi ndo wide
open se
close
hopp ending
certain calls

light
across
the

grass that
grows in

droves off
green

grosues that
removes
in
light like
slight
slender
grasses slim

s u
  i ppose a quest tion
         an atten tod say
                   etails
      tos s lip p errance
                    u
      to say with Poise ture
                         plead
         in sup pl i cation
      in su btl e ap
            pp   lanting
               answer
         in ask   ance s
                gl

w o n e ' t dance
d o t ask
won o t
heartf r e e l t n o d o t hing e s
it should d o ne
d a n ce s k
w oo n ' t
you ?

what was I
staying?
was I trying
to say?
trying to truth to
through say to
sends up
trashly
said
please what was I ry ing
to s say?

Afterword

What does holding back your words and thoughts feel like? What does it look like, this stuckness, these word-opportunities held back, these thought-trails derailed, these thought-tangents caused to diverge? What does it look like for ambivalence and divergence to converge during the moment of articulation, only for several things in parallel to rush in, being expressed all at once? What does it look like when all word-opportunities collide at once, like wildly unspooling threads, like heavy raindrops on a glass surface racing from one fork to the next and merging, like pathways of synapse after synapse firing all at once?

This collection of poems titled *Eke* are poems of aching, of aching towards an expression, of enacting both painful and opportune expression, of words still stuck and struck in a state of percolation, a plasma state of signification. These poems are attempts at articulating, a-tempt-ation towards meaning. The word fragments and the letter displacements in the poems create visual aberrations which visually enact the fumbles and stammers in the attempt at expressing what wishes to be expressed, and nevertheless concedes that complete expression, or a closure in expression, can never be achieved. These fragments and displacements also recreate the mental interjections or the thought-flood of overthinking caused by polysemantic words, ambiguous situations, and hyperactive word-meaning activations.

To eke is to gently ask: Are people who are let in, who stray past these nets, who puncture through these protective barriers, guests or gusts? Do you trust them to stay, do you risk hurting them, do they leave an imprint on your soul? Are these imprints footprints on sand or puncture wounds? Wounds, as in the breaking of the skin; or wounds, as in the bitter taste of metallic twisting?

To eke is to pause and inquire if falling in love with someone means attuning or a tuning to the whispers of the heart. Whose heart? Theirs or yours? Is love a missing 'he' in heart? Is love missing? Is love amassing? Is love an art, in whispers and whisps, or in artful whisperous offings and offerings?

To eke is to step into pool after pool of uncertainties, to step into a pool and to discover it is an ocean, vast and dark, deep and black. And in the darkness and blackness, it is to ask and try to find a way, to make meaning. Unsure, always unsure. Uncertain, always uncertain. Unascertainable sureness. Unassured certainty.

To eke is to be stuck, to be dispossessed, to ask if I am feeling what I am feeling, thinking what I am thinking. Did I think I felt it, or think I thought it? Was it ever there? I took a picture but found it blurry – the subject whizzed by too fast. Did you see it? Did you feel it too? Or am I just imagining it?

To eke is to wonder if you feel the same way, think the same way. Even though logic would dictate that all subjective feelings are subjective, to eke is to hope that you feel and think the same way, to hope that you understand, to hope that you did see what I saw.

To eke is unappealing, but it is a peeling towards peals of trapped uncertainties too soft, too nebulous to be expressed in precise pinpoint words.

To eke is to accept that thoughts, ideas, memories and expression can be intrusive, and to accommodate them in day-to-day life, and carry on thinking, ideating, remembering, and expressing anyway.

To eke is to be a measure braver in a volatile, uncertain, complex, and ambiguous world.

Eke

To eke is to invite you in and let your witnessing, your reading, be a mark on meaning-making so that each poem reaches a form of understanding that, while still not upstanding, is at least a gentle rippling on a surface never still.

Acknowledgements

Eke would not have been possible, and *Eke* would not have been articulated without the guidance and encouragement of Divya Victor and Jennifer Crawford – they understood where I barely understood the value of what I was doing with words, and gave me the confidence to keep exploring. During the course of the exploration of *Eke*, the patient explanations from many kind friends and teachers of the many signs and significations in language, religion, art and literature helped make clear a world of words. Thank you for your graciousness and for the many arrivals of meaning.

The poems "teller", "moodlet", "clooked up", "conflitting" and "resolutely" were formally published in OF ZOOS, Issue 12.1 – P R (I) S E, January 2024. The poems "brontide", "im pluie", "wont dansk" and "moodlet" were presented during the 2023 Gaudy Boy Poetry Prize Finalists Reading, during which the recorded audio version of "moodlet" was first aired. The poems "im pluie", "brontide" and "still mo(u)rning" were formally published in Kitaab.org, 27 May 2019.

About the Author

© Afiqah Tambee

Wahidah Tambee graduated with degrees in psychology and creative writing from Nanyang Technological University.

From the Latin *gaudium*, meaning "joy," Gaudy Boy publishes books that delight readers with the various powers of art. The name is taken from the poem "Gaudy Turnout," by Singaporean poet Arthur Yap, about his time abroad in Leeds, the United Kingdom. Similarly inspired by such diasporic wanderings and migrations, Gaudy Boy brings literary works by authors of Asian heritage to the attention of an American audience and beyond. Established in 2018 as the imprint of the New York City–based literary nonprofit Singapore Unbound, we publish poetry, fiction, and literary nonfiction.

Visit our website at www.singaporeunbound.org/gaudyboy.

Winners of the Gaudy Boy Poetry Book Prize

Fablemaker: Poems
by Mandy Moe Pwint Tu

Interrogation Records: Poems
by Jeddie Sophronius

Waking Up to the Pattern Left by a Snail Overnight: Poems
by Jim Pascual Agustin

Time Regime: Poems
by Jhani Randhawa

Object Permanence: Poems
by Nica Bengzon

Play for Time: Poems
by Paula Mendoza

Autobiography of Horse: A Poem
by Jenifer Sang Eun Park

The Experiment of the Tropics: Poems
by Lawrence Lacambra Ypil

Fiction and Nonfiction

Other Series

From Gaudy Boy Translates

Memorial Club: A Novel
by Mozid Mahmud

Picking off new shoots will not stop the spring:
Witness Poems and Essays from Burma/Myanmar 1988–2021
edited by Ko Ko Thett and Brian Haman

Amanat: Women's Writing from Kazakhstan
edited by Zaure Batayeva and Shelley Fairweather-Vega

Ulirát: Best Contemporary Stories in Translation from the Philippines
edited by Tilde Acuña, John Bengan, Daryll Delgado, Amado Anthony G.
Mendoza III, and Kristine Ong Muslim

Books by our other imprint, Bench Press

Sample and Loop: A Simple History of Singaporeans in America
by Jee Leong Koh

Snow at 5 PM: Translations of an Insignificant Japanese Poet
by Jee Leong Koh

Seven Studies for a Self-Portrait: Poems
by Jee Leong Koh

Equal to the Earth: Poems
by Jee Leong Koh

Lightly in the Good of Day: Poems
by Bob Hart

Try to Have Your Writing Make Sense:
The Quintessential PFFA Anthology: Poems
edited by Donna Smith and Howard Miller